STIFLE THOSE LIMITATIONS

Tashi Browne

Acknowledgements

I am humbled and emotional for this journey as it portrays a very personal and passionate affirmation for me. It is with great pleasure that I recognize a few key people who have made this journey a success and express my gratitude.

My mom, for providing support and modeling excellence so well that living up to her standards and belief in me serves as an energizer for success.

My husband, who has always demonstrated belief in me and my dreams and supports me 100%. His constant motivational reminders that I can be anything I put my mind to always push me to do more and be more.

The first reviewers of this book who shared insights and recommendations for enhancing my thoughts: Lisa Agard, Sonya Forrester and Julia Tohme.

And to you readers; I thank you for taking this journey with me and I do hope the message lights your path.

First published in 2024 by Tashi Browne

© Tashi Browne 2024
The moral rights of the author have been asserted

All rights reserved. Except as permitted under fair use for the purposes of study, research, criticism or review, no part of this book may be reproduced, stored in a retrieval system, communicated or transmitted in any form or by any means without prior written permission. All inquiries should be made to the author.

ISBN: 978-1-923007-41-3

Book production and text design by Publish Central
Cover design by Pipeline Design

The paper this book is printed on is environmentally friendly.

Disclaimer
The material in this publication is of the nature of general comment only, and does not represent professional advice. It is not intended to provide specific guidance for particular circumstances and it should not be relied on as the basis for any decision to take action or not take action on any matter which it covers. Readers should obtain professional advice where appropriate, before making any such decision. To the maximum extent permitted by law, the author and publisher disclaim all responsibility and liability to any person, arising directly or indirectly from any person taking or not taking action based on the information in this publication.

Contents

How to Read this Book   iii

CHAPTER 1: We All Have Dominion Power   1
Lighting the Fire Within   3
Visualizing Dominion   6
Exercising Dominion   7
Being Cautious with Dominion Power   9
What Does Having Dominion Mean for You?   15

CHAPTER 2: The Challenges of Exercising Dominion   19
Eliminating the Darkness   20

CHAPTER 3: Cultivating Your Identity as a Stream to Stifle Limitations   31
It is Up to Us   32
Defining Your Potential   33
Cultivating Your Potential   37

CHAPTER 4: Have Faith in Your Potential	**45**
We Live by Faith Daily	46
From Faith to Achievement	48
Feed FAITH and Fight FEAR	52
CHAPTER 5: Don't Dim Your Light	**57**
Keep Shining	58
Your Keep Shining Platform	60
Shine and Continue to Shine	**71**
References	**73**

How to Read this Book

The evolution of this book has come through my journey of self-doubt and limiting beliefs. I have grown over the years through reading and exposing myself to motivational leaders who have guided my belief system away from personal perspectives based on physical circumstances. There are many instances when we are faced with doubt based on the things we see before us, but it's important we examine who we are and realize we can accomplish the things our heart desires. We can stifle the limiting belief systems we all have and repossess the treasures destined for us.

As I started to find my truest self – based on the need for me to believe in me and in my possibilities – I began to ignore the naysayers and stifle limiting beliefs. This concept of stifling limitations was introduced when I participated in a speech contest as part of Toastmasters International. This message was shared at the Caribbean-level contest, where I shared on self-definition through stifling limitations. I emerged in second place out of thirteen contestants, but the greatest victory was the overwhelming encouragement and feedback on how the message touched so many in the audience. Based on that premise, I felt a passion within to expand on this concept by writing this book. This book aims to motivate people who are stuck because of limitations, and to encourage that YOU are able to achieve the idea that is within your being. YOU can represent your authentic self and let your light shine. This can be achieved by recognizing you have **Dominion Power** (the right to control limitations), and that power, once activated, will allow you to see your limitations from a proactive perspective. This helps you carve a path to stifle these limitations through self-definition and potential determination. With Faith, your potential will be harnessed, and you can walk into your light of success. As you bask in the beauty of that light, always remember to shine, shine, shine.

Use this book as a stepping stone to acknowledge what your limitations are, and to unleash the giant within you to stifle them at all costs so you can live an abundant life.

The path for stifling limitations is depicted through the following illustration, and this book unfolds this concept in a simple manner so you can have the courage to 'let your light shine'. At the end of each chapter, there are reflective questions to assist you in being intentional during this journey. Be committed to completing the questions as you progress to that place of release.

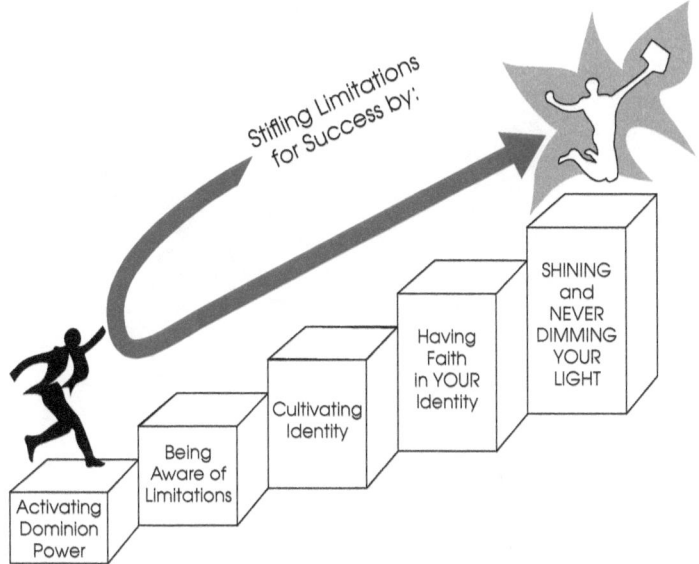

CHAPTER 1

We All Have Dominion Power

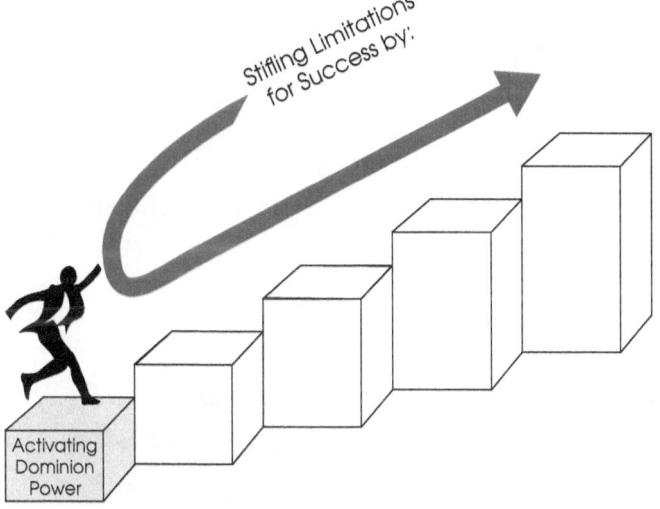

'There is no passion in playing small, settling for a life less than the one we are capable of living.'

Nelson Mandela

Genesis 1:27–28

So God created mankind in his own image,
in the image of God he created them;
male and female he created them.

God blessed them and said to them, 'Be fruitful and increase in number; fill the earth and subdue it. **Rule** over the fish in the sea and the birds in the sky and over every living creature that moves on the ground.'
King James Version[1]

God commanded us to have dominion. His first pronouncement to man was that of dominion – he formulated us to dominate.

Dominion speaks to sovereignty and control, and the scripture clearly outlines that we have been given instructions to be limitless since we have control over the earth, waters and every living creature. The scripture *Psalms 115:16*, which states, 'The heaven, even the heavens, are the Lord's: but the earth hath he given to the children of men,'[1] also demonstrates that dominion over the earth is our birthright. Therefore, our behaviors, mindset, attitudes, purpose, driven nature and need for attainment should be diverse, abundant, fearless and limitless to synchronize with our Dominion Power – our Dominion Delegated Authority.

God provided us with the innate ability to rule and reign, so our drive should always be to achieve victory. Based on this premise, we need to be cognizant of the power of God and know that he would not give us this ability without directions for success. God will equip us to exercise our dominion mandate once we submit to his free will for dominion, and it is because of this that we have the power to rule and reign and we can use this power over any limitation. Innate within us is that dominating spirit that should be recognized as a powerful force in our daily lives. As we activate the spirit of dominion, we release the spirit of fear, mediocrity and limitations, and cause the spirit of Faith and abundance to rise.

Lighting the Fire Within

Dominance is not about being in an autocratic position, but is solely based on having responsibility – it allows an individual to take care of the earth by harnessing its resources as well as protecting them while achieving one's innate potential. Dominion is not the authority to work *against* God's creation, but the ability to work *for* it. This means we are not aggressive and arrogant about our innate power, but we use that power as a force to light the fire within and be successful because of our nature to dominate.

Dominion implies we have power over LIMITATIONS since we have been given purpose on earth by God, and nothing should stop us from realizing and living that purpose because we can tap into our dominion quality and live above earthly limitations. If we want to live dominion, we need to make ourselves worthy of it so it will be attracted to us. If we deny our power to dominate then we allow the power of limits to encompass us. The poem *Achievement* by Ella Wheeler Wilcox speaks the truth of Dominion Power by demonstrating that dominion is within us awaiting our command to set it free.

Achievement

Trust in thine own untried capacity
As thou wouldst trust in God Himself.
Thy soul
Is but an emanation from the whole.
Thou dost not dream what forces lie in thee,
Vast and unfathomed as the grandest sea.
Thy silent mind o'er diamond caves may roll,

> Go seek them—but let pilot will control
> Those passions which thy favouring winds can be.
> No man shall place a limit in thy strength;
> Such triumphs as no mortal ever gained
> May yet be thine if thou wilt but believe
> In thy Creator and thyself. At length
> Some feet will tread all heights now unattained—
> Why not thine own? Press on! achieve! achieve![2]

Dominion cannot work on its own; we must do the things necessary to activate it, to initiate it. If we start with limits in our minds we stagnate the activation, but if we are aware of those limits and activate our Dominion Power, we release our potential.

The opening line of that poem speaks to belief and attainment of things one is made of but one needs to trust, as the line states, '... *in thine own untried capacity*'. To trust in the hidden capacity means recognizing that it's in our nature to dominate. We have the innate ability to conquer all the fears that will prevent us from believing in this capacity as we recognize we have the spirit to rule over those limiting beliefs. The closing line demonstrates the need to question the opposition by asking 'why NOT me?', and as soon as the opposition gives an answer, we tap into that spirit to dominate and overcome the opposition's need for us to remain average and not realize our potential.

The force of the opposition is to oppress us and make us believe that settling for what we see in the physical is all we can be. However, as we visualize our greatest self, we permit ourselves to rule over our thoughts and actions to get to that place we deem successful.

Visualizing Dominion

A visit to the riverine areas of Region 9 Guyana afforded me the opportunity to visualize my own dominion. One day, I and five other passengers were on a boat sailing down the Rupununi River, when suddenly the boat's engine got caught in a seine. I experienced a moment of dead panic as I was wearing no lifejacket and I could not swim. The boat's engine stopped immediately, and the boat proceeded to float down the Rupununi. The captain tried - with no visible sign of panic - to cut the tangled seine from the engine.

At that moment, the power of limitation penetrated my thoughts: 'You have **no** lifejacket and you cannot swim!' it screamed loudly in my overheating head. This reality was startling as I stared at the surrounding water with tears in my eyes; afraid and trembling. Then the power of dominion whispered: dominion cannot work in us if we do not activate it.

That was a major defining path for designing my life.

In essence, how would I have been able to ensure my survival when I had never practiced the basic skill of swimming and I was in an environment that required that skill? We have Dominion Power for success, but we need to equip ourselves for that power to operate.

It is easy to believe, 'I have the power to control my situation,' however, control will only work when we activate it. Think about driving a car - we can never have control over the motion and speed of that car if we do not have the skills to initially accelerate. Dominion Power says that I have the power; but the power will only work when I recognize I have the power and I *activate* that power.

Dominion means I place myself in positions to be exposed for my acceleration; I equip myself with the necessary skills so I can put those skills to work and activate my hidden powers.

Exercising Dominion

When an individual has Dominion Power, that power is used to take charge of any circumstance in their life. They can use that power to dominate their environment instead of allowing the environment to dominate them.

A man who claims that his father left his mother, and his grandfather left his grandmother, and it is a chain impossible for him to break – and so that's his reason for leaving his wife and children – denies the power of dominion.

A woman who comes from a family where every husband is unfaithful to their wife and admits that she doesn't expect her husband to be different denies the power of dominion.

A woman who believes that her worth is dependent on the opinions of others and the cosmetic nature of beauty denies the power of dominion.

Dominion shouts *I am not a result of my circumstances, but I am the result of what I create.*

Life is sometimes described as a battle, and as we strive to exercise dominion, limitations scare us. That is reality. Limitations outline to us our shortcomings; they shout about our failures of the past and our possible failures in the future. Limitations say to us that risks are not worth taking. However, the world really and truly is for the TAKING – it is for us to live out our most authentic selves. When we exercise dominion, we first acknowledge that limitations exist and we are willing to do everything in our power to stifle them.

We are attacking the issue from its root and not ignoring its presence.

Defining limitations is examined more in chapter 2. When we are aware of our limitations, we can utilize them as a fuel to drive our success. With our Dominion Power at the core telling us we do not need to allow these limitations to prevent us from achieving our goals, our Dominion Power will be our fortress to conquer the perceived untouchable, unattainable, impossible situations before us.

Ask yourself – what can I do differently to change my socially expected script? The answer is to exercise dominion in the areas where you feel uncertainty.

Being Cautious with Dominion Power

Recognizing your Dominion Power should not lead you to a place lacking humility because this will be detrimental to your success. Operating in your Dominion Power is not a hall pass for arrogance or high-handed behavior. In fact, if not managed carefully, we could start to become self-absorbed to the point of cutting off feedback and input we need from others. We begin to falsely believe that it is all about us and as such we operate in a selfish, arrogant manner. This lack of caution will hamper our success since our dominance needs to work in unison with our environment. People around us must derive benefits from the power we have and not be drained by it. The Dominion Power within us is not to operate arrogantly but appropriately for success that serves us and others around us.

The sinful nature of man uses dominion wrongly in some instances as it is seen as an authoritative mistreatment of nature and life. We are called to exhibit our Dominion Power rightly by upholding good values and not being destructive. We are called to recognize that there is more than enough for all of us, visible and invisible. Our every action should be for service, and done responsibly. We are to serve others by seeking to meet their best interests while focusing on our need to meet our own interests with the aim of an abundance mentality that there is room for all.

The Dominion Power within us is like the faith of the mustard seed. It is to be used to work for God and not against God. It says, '*I can move any mountain*' – but it remembers that these mountains were created by our heavenly Father and so that movement does not destroy his glory but works for his glory.

We examine Psalm 27:1-3 which states:

> The LORD is my light and my salvation—whom shall I fear?
> The LORD is the stronghold of my life—of whom shall I be afraid?
> When the wicked advance against me to devour me, it is my enemies and my foes who will stumble and fall.
> Though an army besiege me, my heart will not fear; though war break out against me, even then I will be confident.

This declarative prayer sends a message of the type of confidence that needs to rise up in times of struggle, in times of failure, in times of fear. This confidence activates our **will** to exercise our dominion to overpower our limitations. The confidence assists us in knowing that we should not underestimate the power of the holy spirit to guide us and to recognize the sovereignty of God's power over all the world.

Our Dominion Power says we will make every effort in seeking to control circumstances that seek to defeat us. George Bernard Shaw nicely depicts why dominion becomes important with the words, 'this is the true joy of life: the being used up for a purpose recognized by yourself as a mighty one; being a force of nature instead of a feverish, selfish little clot of ailments and grievances, complaining that the world will not devote itself to making you happy.'

Relatable Dominion Story

This story has motivated me and allowed me to attribute the concept of dominion as alive, active and authentic.

The first time I stumbled upon the name Lisa Nichols was during the phase when I was tired and emotional about my hair. This period was one where the entire back of my head was almost bald and I was plaiting and wearing wigs a lot to hide that shame. However, I was at a place where I wanted a release from that bondage. I came across a video by this remarkable woman, who shared her story of loving herself and strategically planning a release for her life. That first video changed my hair journey, as I did a tapered hairstyle to regrow my hair and renew my love for myself. Today braiding and wigs are used as a form of my hair expression and not as a form of bondage. I stepped boldly into the world unashamed – confident to live my authentic life and not be limited by my appearance.

The main aspect that stood out in her story for me was her active need to dominate her circumstances and her life.

Amid our struggles, we can't see clearly but we can always strive for clarity to reap success. It is not clarity alone that will help us but trust in an outcome, and Lisa Nichols had trust.

During an interview on the *Steve Harvey Show*, Nichols genuinely shared her story. She was a single mother on government assistance with insufficient funds in her bank account, raising a son whose dad was in prison. One day she couldn't afford to buy pampers for her son – she needed to wrap him in a towel, which she described as a rock-bottom feeling. That moment defined her now successful life as she actively allowed her Dominion Power to operate. Her defining words were, 'I have to be my own rescue. No one's going to rescue me.'[3] Her change parameters included:

- Her realization that she couldn't grow with people who were struggling just like her. She needed to let a few people go so she could return to help them – she couldn't help them with her struggle but with her strength.
- She attended conferences that would add value to her personal solutions – she attended a conference 42 times just to ensure she got it right.

- With the job she got after her rock-bottom feeling, she used each paycheck to save for her future by depositing through the theme 'Funding my Dream,' with no idea what that dream entailed.

Her Dominion Power translated to meaning that she needed to rescue herself, and when her dream was ready to come alive she would be equipped to live that dream.

It is not about what we have now but what we trust we can have. For dominion to work in us we must recognize we have the power and activate it.

Lisa Nichols is the founder of Motivating the Masses, a platform for personal and professional development. She has understood her Dominion Power and has transitioned from not being able to afford pampers to transforming lives around the world.

If you haven't heard about this remarkable woman, be sure to check her out and learn more at www.motivatingthemasses.com.

You can remain stuck in your limitations, or you can do uncomfortable things to accomplish what your heart desires.

What Does Having Dominion Mean for You?

To have dominion means you must understand your power and develop strength in that power. Your strength must be both aggressive and proactive so that when limitations appear you can remain grounded in your power. You need to ensure you are indeed strong and not just *acting* strong, because when you act strong and the limitations come – you will crumble.

Dominion will represent a path of identifying your strength so you become a conqueror. Dominion Power will be threatened as you are fighting against real forces that seek to stifle your fullest potential. As you recognize this reality, you must always be armored so your defense is strong and impenetrable. The Bible demonstrates this strength acquisition by indicating we should have a strategy to win focusing on our resources to win – these include:

- Belt of Truth: which will allow us to always remember who we are and the value our power has.
- Shield of Faith: this allows us the authority to trust in our Dominion Power.

For deeper reflection on this strength acquisition, read Ephesians 6:10-20.

> *Understand that you have the power to dominate over your circumstances. Activate that power.*

Chapter Reflection

1. Determine two areas in your life that you are intimidated by and focus on how you can have dominion over those areas.

Area	Your dominion plan
1.	
2.	

2. Create a statement or mantra to consistently remind yourself of your Dominion Power.
   Example: 'Dominion is my Heritage.'

Chapter Nuggets

- Be aware you have the power to dominate and celebrate that awareness.
- Visualize what you can do to operate in dominion, since visualizing motivates.
- Commence your journey to exercise that Dominion Power by taking steps that activate the power.
- Remember to always use your Dominion Power wisely.

CHAPTER 2

The Challenges of Exercising Dominion

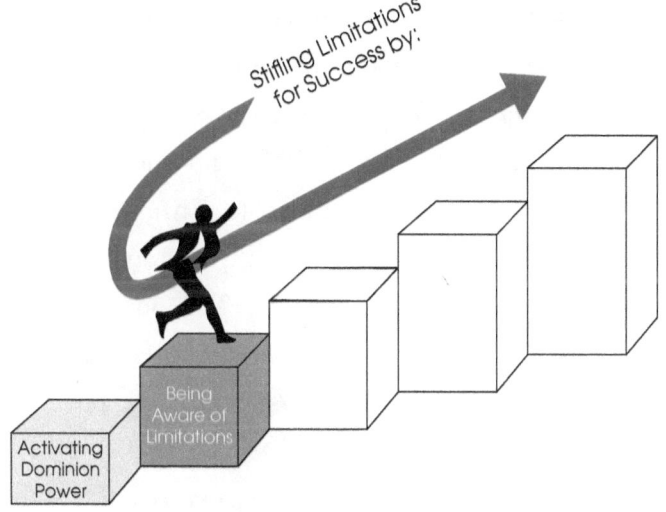

'Light that is continuously surrounded by darkness is in danger of losing its brilliance.'

Myles Munroe

Eliminating the Darkness

Exercising our Dominion Power will require some work, because as we prepare to launch ourselves, our fears and inadequacies will stare at us and intimidate us. As we allow these limiting thoughts, resources and ideas to surround us, we inhibit the light within from shining. It is our prerogative to eliminate the darkness (limitations) so that our light (dreams, passions and purpose) can brighten the world.

A limited person is a restricted individual who suffers when he/she cannot achieve the desires of his/her heart. Though one may see or know where he/she belongs, or what he/she should attain, one may find it difficult to get there because of the things that intimidate. That person finds it hard to believe that he/she is worthy and does not truly embrace what he/she was created for. The individual lacks the compassion to treat themselves as an asset for the success they so envision. Deep within, he/she denies the possibility of a reality of the desired success that is within reach.

One of the indications of a destiny that is stifled is that the owner of such a destiny suffers limitations in his/her life. To be limitless, we need to first be aware of the things that scare us, and confront these things. Until we stifle the things that limit us, we will remain restricted in every sphere of life.

Aspirations do not determine achievement; implementation does. And to implement means to fight against any deterrent that sits in the way of our achievements. Myles Munroe posited that 'nothing is more irritating, guilt-producing and incriminating, than an unfinished book, product, goal etc. Live to your last chapter'.[1] We need to carve the life we desire by facing the fears that are on fire and not being imprisoned. Everyone who wants to enter his/her destiny must be free from this spirit of limitation. The path to destiny is never guaranteed to be smooth but the fight for arrival to that place of bliss makes the obstacle-filled path worthwhile.

Overcoming a Scarcity Mindset

We should shift our thinking to a place that pushes us beyond our barriers. We are often too overwhelmed by our scarcity mentality – we believe that we do not have enough resources, enough sleep, enough time. We always burden ourselves with not having enough, and that mindset holds us back since we think from a place of lack.

This scarcity mindset demonstrates our cognitive nature to revert to limitations and we deprive ourselves by believing we are not capable of more, we are not good enough, we are not worthy. When we recognize and accept these limitations as real and as a way for us to protect ourselves from being vulnerable or being exposed to failure, we must strive to stifle them and push forward to our success.

These limitations tell us we are not ready for the next big avenue in our lives and we set out to achieve perfection, to be completely secure and maybe invincible before walking into our light – we try to play it safe. The reality is that we may never get to that place of perfection amid our limitations, but we can create the synergies to find avenues to stifle the things that seem to control us. This will allow us to be creative in our endeavors to be purpose-driven and all that we were meant to be. We need to dare ourselves to show up and achieve our wildest dreams. Observing our limitations should serve to bring us into better awareness of what may hamper our success, so we can design strategies to overcome those. Limitations should not be viewed as barriers to our growth, but rather as stepping stones to realizing our purpose.

Viewing the Negative as an Opportunity

It may be true that we do not have enough for the results we desire in our present state. However, the acknowledgement of this lack should not be a place we dwell in. Instead, it should be a moment for us to determine how we can rise above the lack and be creative in our prospects for results. If we live in the negative attributes of life, it is difficult to arrive at the positive end. But when we view the negative as an opportunity to work towards accomplishment, positive results are sure.

It is obvious that limits exist and are as real as the air we breathe. Limitations can appear in the form of toxic people, sickness, lack of resources, childhood experiences, physical appearance, educational background – and the list goes on. They are anything that tramples our belief in the possibilities that exist within us. But limitations should be viewed as a phase to reach liberation – the phase that strengthens you and does not stagnate you.

For instance, lack of finance can be the limitation that we face to move ahead in starting our dream business. As we acknowledge that limit, we can organize a strategy to overcome it. How about striving to be better managers of our financial resources to arrive at that dream? What about seeking funding opportunities to arrive at that dream? Knowing our limits is powerful in pushing us to activate our Dominion Power to overcome these limits.

We have the power within us to overcome any challenges we observe or imagine and redesign our perspective by selecting a regime that matches our intentions for success. If we don't give ourselves the power to launch out, we will never know the power within. It is usually easier to sit on our throne of limitations and list all the challenges and barriers, but if we can only give ourselves permission to WIN, we set ourselves apart.

Relatable Dominion Story

My major challenge during childhood was my size, and it limited me because others recognized my deficiency in muscularity and body mass, and some had descriptions for me. Names such as: bones, magga girl, a bag a bones and a pint a blood were a few of the images attributed to me. It caused tears to flow in quiet moments as I hated that I was so skinny. I was not always bold enough to participate in activities because I didn't feel beautiful.

In many ways it felt like society was defining me as an outsider, but I later recognized that self-definition is key to success. If I can't define who I am then I open the doors to accept everyone else's definition of me. Society's opinion of a person's identity is always going to be based on a category or stereotype. I had to realize the power of defining who I was and who I wanted to be. I had to understand that to live a life that means something I must find a way of working out the obstacles and embracing who I am, then it will work remarkably in my favor.

> And remarkably it did. As I stifled limiting beliefs, I was able to love myself for who I am. My reality is that even today I am slim – but I have strength in my slimness.

Defining Who You Are

Myles Munroe said it nicely: 'The wealthiest place in the world is not the gold mines of South America or the oil fields of Iraq or Iran. They are not the diamond mines of South Africa or the banks of the world. The wealthiest place on the planet is just down the road. It is the cemetery. There lie buried companies that were never started, inventions that were never made, bestselling books that were never written, and masterpieces that were never painted. In the cemetery is buried the greatest treasure of untapped potential.'[2]

But WHY? Why is this so?

This is so because people allow others to define who they are. It is time we discover our true identity – remove the limits we place on ourselves and strive to be the best *us* we can. And how can we do this? By STIFLING limitations.

My journey to finding myself began when I joined Toastmasters International in 2014 (a non-profit educational organization that teaches public speaking and leadership skills through a worldwide network of clubs). It allowed me to unleash my voice, and as I started speaking there was a fire within that was burning fiercely and my soul was filled with satisfaction. I started to activate my potential and shine regardless of my perceived darkness (being skinny). The result of this unleashing was that audiences loved me. Amazingly, we stifle the power we have to shine due to being fearful of the outcomes - and the outcomes usually are contrary. We need to be brave and bold to explore the perceived darkness so we can observe and walk in the glorious light that really exists.

We all have a spark within us that has the potential to become light. Light for nations to see, light for eternity. This potential when not activated lies dormant, hidden within our souls, strength and beauty that sits unmarred by our limitations. We need to become the person we have not seen and unleash our powers. We need to utilize the things we have in our hands and create our masterpiece.

The lesson here is that limitations exist, they are real, and we need to be aware of that. It is important for us to identify what limitations exist within our life and seek strategies to stifle them. Do not be ignorant of the limitations that surround you - identify them but do not OWN them - they are not yours to keep. When you identify a limitation, do everything in your power to stifle it.

Relatable Dominion Story

When we think of our limitations and how we can stifle them — it is important we recognize some of them we CANNOT remove. We can re-adjust our attitudes through our identity as a form of stifling. Identity definition will be examined in chapter 3. While some of them we CAN clearly eliminate — the goal is to identify what limits our actions for success and how we will stifle these limits from rising up against our success.

My biggest struggle was with being too slim, and from time to time I would read stories of people who had stuttered, grew up in extreme poverty or were even born with a deformity. All these challenges may slow an individual's ability to operate effectively, but we are all gifted with talents and skills that are valuable. We need to know and believe that the world needs what we have to give because we are enough.

Grow to be as boundless as the wind and as unstoppable as a powerful flood.

Chapter Reflection

1. Identify specific limitations that exist within your life by focusing on every aspect: physical, spiritual, emotional and mental. Link these limitations to specific goals you have set.

Personal goals	Limitations			
	Physical	Spiritual	Emotional	Mental

2. Consider possible strategies to stifle the limitations listed above.

   List your strategies here:

Chapter Nuggets

- Be not afraid to identify your limitations.
- Research and define possible strategies to overcome those limitations.
- Recognize that the limitations should be your fuel and not your fortress.

CHAPTER 3

Cultivating Your Identity as a Stream to Stifle Limitations

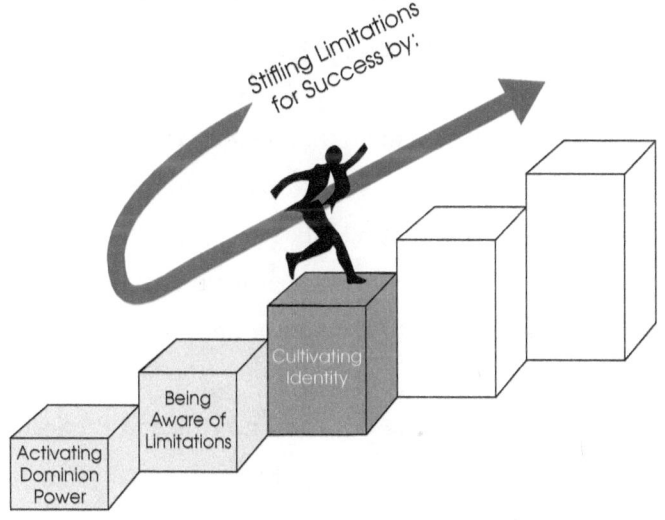

'Somewhere – something intelligent is waiting to be known.'

Carl Sagan

Limitations can be seen as an excruciating phenomenon, but how else can one win and lead themselves to an exquisite experience? This can only be accomplished by generating ideas to stifle those limitations and winning regardless. Even if your situation may not be ideal, it won't last for long if you see an opportunity and work toward achieving it. You cannot travel to your determined success without stifling the things that hold you back. When you accept the presence of these shortcomings, you are then tasked with envisioning possibilities to win despite the odds.

It is Up to Us

We can all ignore our limitations and not achieve our desires because of the way we think. It is up to us to decide what we want to cultivate in our minds about ourselves – we have the choice to see who we want to be. It is up to us to imagine fearlessly or visualize with limits magnified – whichever way we decide, we create.

The interaction between a human being and the secrets of inspiration is called *creativity*. In this context, it is the ability to view one's circumstances and derive ideas to achieve success despite the circumstances. It says I CAN BE OR ACHIEVE ANYTHING in spite of my fortunes or failures – in spite of my strengths or struggles – in spite of my power or pain. We can recognize that situations in which we reside do not prevent us from achieving or do not allow us to achieve. It all has to do with our willingness to use the mysteries of inspiration to derive our success.

To activate our creativity for success, we need to:

- define our potential
- cultivate our potential.

This will be achieved through our 'in-nergies' – a term coined to indicate that for us to derive a benefit despite circumstances there needs to be power from within. The force that pushes you in the direction that is compelled by your inner being. The inner strength that is on fire to shine – charged with energy that is durable. We all have in-nergy but we need to trigger it to work.

Defining Your Potential

Casting Crowns – a contemporary Christian rock band – use the words 'we were made for so much more than ordinary lives. We were made for more than just survival – we were made to thrive' in the song titled *Thrive*.[1] These words allow us to recognize the innate attribute of understanding who we are so we can be all that we have the potential to be.

To identify who we are – we need to define our potential through:

- relevance and novelty
- asking the right questions
- persistence.

Relevance and Novelty

The quality of a state of being demonstrates one's relevance, while being unique and original demonstrates one's novelty.

Relevance ensures that we tell ourselves: what I am capable of is important in addressing a situation/challenge/need. My unique touch to the process will exhibit my originality and differences, allowing novelty to be demonstrated.

Novelty ensures that when you know who you are and what you have to offer, you are motivated to move in a direction that forms a stream to stifle limitations. Novelty allows you to set aside the time needed to take a step back and explore the unique ways of doing something.

It is important to evaluate ourselves based on strengths and weaknesses to derive our interests and the needs we can fulfill to tap into our identity to portray our potential.

Relevance puts your potential in context while novelty aligns your personality to that context for presentation.

Questions

Ask questions as a trigger to assist you in defining your potential. Questioning and curiosity are building blocks for your potential to be evolved and realized. Interesting questions that assist with this process would be questions that eliminate constraints – for example: what if money was not a parameter for success in a particular area – what would you do?

When you ask questions that have no constraints, it assists you in identifying your potential. Questioning puts you in a place where you are less vulnerable, and you give yourself authority and power over the situation. Finding solutions to the questions you ask yourself liberates you and pushes forth your potential like a seedling protruding through the soil into the light. You create new exposure for yourself and you bring forth your potential, ready to bear fruit as it continues to mature.

Persistence

Persistence is another trigger to assist you in defining your potential. Once there is an innate interest in a direction, being persistent and consistent with your actions will help you to craft the path while defining your potential.

Relatable Dominion Story

In November 2017, I made a conscious decision that it was time for me to switch jobs. Based on questioning, I recognized that I was capable and worthy of working in a manner that could lead to global impact. This process commenced with a specific goal in mind and was challenged by several rejections, failed interviews, and non-responses from organizations. Throughout the journey I applied to thirteen organizations before receiving that final yes in September 2018. That same persistence has allowed me to define a new potential involving writing, speaking and teaching, on my conviction that regardless of the stones thrown at us, we can stifle limitations and be all that we strive to be. With that persistence, my potential to share this message as I write this book is inspiring and motivating me further.

Cultivating Your Potential

We all need to have the ability to see our potential operating beyond our imagination. As it is written in the Bible, we are created to showcase the potential that our God has prepared for us in advance – so our potential is innate since the beginning of time. All that is required of us is that we identify it, activate it and continuously sharpen it, so we can reap success continually.

As we nurture our potential, it's important for us to recognize three key areas that play a critical role in the enhancement of that potential:

- responsibility
- effort and value
- growth mindset.

Responsibility

We are all responsible for the evolution of our potential, and as a result it is our obligation – it is all up to us; therefore, we need to stretch ourselves and enhance ourselves through **ambition, ability** and **commitment**.

With ambition – we can be both aware and intentional so that we can take responsibility for our potential. Awareness helps us to make it our right to know what our potential requires to meet its highest level, while being intentional represents our goal to always make the best of every moment as it unfolds.

With ability - we allow ourselves to be as absorbing as possible with what we can do and allow our creativity to be as varied as possible so that we can review it later for relevance and practicality. This ability sets forth all ideas and intentions that we are capable of manifesting.

With commitment - we stay true to the path of cultivating and developing the identity created through observation, networking, and experimenting. We observe every moment, being careful to note that sometimes it is better to be silent and reap the wealth of information that is available in that quietness. This level of commitment will push us to greater heights as we become disciplined and learn the art of when to observe versus when to contribute. This will ensure we can maximize the lessons to be learned in every moment. When we network consistently, we take responsibility for our potential by accelerating our talents and or skills through linkages with others. And as we develop ourselves, we must be committed to continually testing the waters so we can fully launch out when we are ready.

Based on us having responsibility we will be able to cultivate our potential and see continued replication.

Effort and Value

Cultivating our potential means that we understand cultivation is an expense at the cost of time, energy, and passion. Do the thing you fear and the death of fear is certain. Being willing to make every effort to cultivate potential speaks volumes, as mere intention does not bear fruit but actual effort does. Valuing the causative nature of man and recognizing the effect this cause will have adds to the cultivation path. This is likely to be the case as it motivates the implementer to work diligently in the land of potential. The rewards of the workmanship are the destination to motivate the cultivation.

We need to see effort and value as investments to enhance our potential. Our effort becomes valuable when we see every action we take as an opportunity to take us closer to a goal. It allows us to understand the importance of intentionality. The origin of the following words is unknown but the message regarding effort and value is priceless:

To realize the value of ONE YEAR, ask a student who failed a grade.

To realize the value of ONE MONTH, ask a mother who gave birth to a premature baby.

To realize the value of ONE WEEK, ask the editor of a weekly newspaper.

To realize the value of ONE DAY, ask the person who was born on February 29th.

To realize the value of ONE HOUR, ask the lovers who are waiting to meet.

To realize the value of ONE MINUTE, ask a person who missed the train.

To realize the value of ONE SECOND, ask a person who just avoided an accident.

To realize the value of ONE MILLISECOND, ask the person who won a silver medal in the Olympics.

Your effort is important as it adds value to what your potential will be.

Growth Mindset

Changing your thought processes and looking at ways to push past barriers and chart new territories is the foundation of a growth mindset. This means we look beyond talent and recognize the need for holistic functioning through body, mind, soul, and spirit, and seek to enhance each aspect so we can really allow the potential we have to come forth full force.

There is a gap between what we currently know and what we need to know, and the key to both growth and happiness is how we respond or use that space. GROWING is the decision we make to cultivate our potential, by recognizing that it is not the rewards garnered which mark our destination but a continuous process to keep producing more.

The person who cannot change the foundation of his thoughts will never be able to change the experience of his life. It is our responsibility to always sharpen what we know to keep adding to the existence of our current rewards for more and more results.

The mind always tries to complete what it pictures, so cultivate your potential by endlessly sharpening your skills.

This lesson speaks to knowing who we are and using that knowledge to stifle limitations. To know who we are, we must identify our potential for ourselves and not leave it at the whims of society.

Clearly have a process where you define yourself. That definition today may not be at the place you want it to be, but it will develop an avenue for you to define your truest self and live that authentic life. The life you live can be created by you or by someone else – you get to choose who the inventor of your life will be.

> *Define your potential, cultivate it and let it be your drive to stifling limitations.*

Chapter Reflection

1. Document who you are currently and who you would like to be.

   (This definition serves as your relevance.)

2. Evaluate the gaps that exist between the current you and the future you.

   Define how you can arrive at the YOU desired within your heart.

   (This definition allows novelty and questioning to be operational.)

Chapter Nuggets

- Be not afraid to define and cultivate your potential.
- Let your uniqueness motivate your success.
- Nurture the defined potential that was planted to reap the harvest.

CHAPTER 4

Have Faith in Your Potential

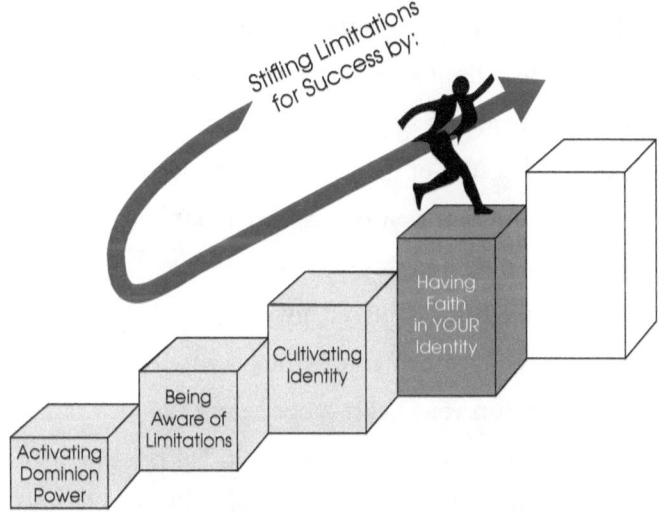

'Now Faith is the substance of things hoped for,
the evidence of things not seen.'

Hebrews 11:1

We Live by Faith Daily

Faith is the fundamental premise of life because we live by Faith daily, even though it might be unconscious. As we get out of our beds in the morning – it is by Faith that we believe the floor will not collapse under our feet. As we eat our breakfast – it is by Faith that we believe we will not be poisoned. As we progress through our days – we apply Faith in the success of things for our lives.

This inherent characteristic becomes magnified and exaggerated as a limitation when we apply it to our dreams, our potential, and our successes. We tend to believe that it is not possible because of its novelty. Then our potential that was defined and that we were excited about becomes stifled due to our own weaknesses of belief.

When something is placed in your heart, you need to recognize it is a desire to come true because realities always start as an idea in your heart – but before the idea can be a reality you need to put your Faith in it. Faith is confidence in things we hope for, so affirm it – visualize it – believe it and it will realize itself. There will always be a gap between your ability and what you want to achieve, and to fill that gap – FAITH is needed.

You need to create a path that allows you to focus on

whom you want to become, and trust in that outcome by believing in your in-nergies. Focus on the purpose of the process and not the pain of the process.

The Bible sets FAITH up in such a way that it is not what you are believing in but WHO you are believing in. Examine the scripture surrounding Peter walking on the water (Matthew 14:22-33).[1]

This message from Peter demonstrates FAITH in action, but stifled. You see FAITH requires a continuous process – even in the midst of the storm when things seem impossible, we need to keep our eyes on the water. Keep our belief in our ideas because Faith is what moves mountains. Matthew 17:20 says: 'Truly I tell you, if you have Faith as small as a mustard seed, you can say to this mountain, "Move from here to there," and it will move. Nothing will be impossible for you.'

Lots of times we won't get into the boat without a safety net – without a plan B – and that's where our shortcoming of achievement is seen because we don't put all our hope in the process and in our potential. Many people have the potential – they know they do, but they stifle that potential because they lack FAITH in their own potential.

The path of FAITH is not an easy one as it requires one to operate in ways that are deemed uncomfortable, unfamiliar, and vulnerable, but PAIN must never be the disqualifier for you to achieve your PURPOSE.

One may say, 'I want to speak and make a global impact in the world' – that individual may have an awesome voice – great motivational skills – confidence – apt. However – they may think, how will it happen? Nobody in my family ever did it, what if no one likes me, why do I think I can do it? ... all Faithless notions that keep the potential untapped.

From Faith to Achievement

As we identify our potential, it is imperative that we develop Faith in that potential – it is the Faith that will push us to the achievement of our heart's desire. To be able to receive the greatest rewards from having Faith, we need to practice three simple methods:

- visualize
- actualize
- realize.

The Bible portrays **visualization** nicely by positing in Habakkuk 2:2: 'Write the vision and make it plain on tablets, that he may run who reads it'. When we write down our vision, we begin the process of its reality. In chapter 3 I talked about identifying your potential – knowing who you are and what you can do. It's important to write this down so that you are able to see very plainly the beauty of your possibilities.

Actualizing is being intentional about your vision – acting upon the dream you see. At times it may sound crazy – but you believe in it anyway. That is Faith – having hope in the things not yet seen.

Realizing is more of living the vision: once you start actualizing you will lead yourself to a point of materializing the outcome – moving from your weakness to a point where you won.

Relatable Dominion Story

I mentioned in chapter 3 my transition into a new job after applying to more than 10 organizations within a nine-month period. During the phase of continually attending interviews and being unsuccessful I decided to examine my Faith in the process. I realized that I was applying for jobs, but I was not resource ready if I did get a job. Sometimes we desire things but we are not prepared to receive them. As I had this revelation, I ventured into purchasing work items as it was my belief that when I get that job – based on my visioning – I would be well-equipped for it. At my old office, I kept packing away things and operating with a shifting mentality, as I started to actualize the reality that I wanted to achieve.

Actualizing also occurred for me through the notion of not committing to the long-term vision of my previous organization. In the midst of my actualizing phase, I was approached to go on a three-month work exchange in India, and I indicated I was unavailable for that mission. When we put Faith in what we see, distractions will come to try to deter our Faith through dangling carrots for us to eat – but FAITH must remain relevant and consistent.

The problem with most of us is that having the idea and the identified potential is not enough because we do not believe in it. We do not recognize that we can be the exception. Maybe there is no one we know who did the thing we want to do, or maybe we know someone whose path was unsuccessful – but it is important to note that previous patterns are not a prediction for what will happen in our lives. For your potential to be relevant, you must have FAITH in it.

Start your Faith process by:

- Writing your vision down. It takes Faith to write what you have in your heart with the expectation of accomplishment. When you write this, write from the notion of who you are. What does your identity say about you? Are you confident? Driven? Organized? Worthy? Then write your vision based on what your identity demonstrates.
- Acting in the direction of the vision. Vision means movement – it will not be accomplished if you don't work for it. Some people believe that it is enough to just write it down. *No*. Your Faith needs to take you a step further to where you start acting for success. Let's say you want to start a business. You write the plan down. You have no location or finances yet, but with Faith you start checking out locations. Setting meetings with real-estate agents – having conversations about your preferred set-up. The person involved in the transaction doesn't have to know that you are just sniffing around with no money 😉. Your action helps to draw reality closer.
- Realizing the vision is yours. OWN it. Live that vision to your fullest potential and leave no room for mediocrity.

I once heard a story where a man indicated his wife would drive into the driveways of luxury homes just to experience what it would feel like when she gets to that place. Their finances didn't match her imagination, but her FAITH did. As you operate you will draw the vision to you, so operate in alignment with that vision.

> Two natures beat within my breast.
> The one is foul, the one is blessed.
> The one I love, the one I hate.
> The one I feed will dominate.
> – *Anonymous*

Feed FAITH and Fight FEAR

A Story of Faith in One's Potential[2]

The late Dr. Myles Munroe was well-known around the world for his leadership and spiritual teachings through keynote speaking, seminars, and books. His journey commenced with lots of limiting words spoken to him by a high school teacher, such as: he was retarded, he looked like a monkey and he was too unsophisticated to learn. He shared these insulting words with his mom, who told him to never believe those descriptions and to live according to the words of Ephesians 3:20, which stated: 'Now unto him that is able to do exceedingly abundantly above all that we ask or think, according to the power that worketh in us'. That scripture changed his perspective on life, as he realized his potential was not determined by the words of the teacher but by what was within himself – he journeyed on a path to educate himself by all means possible. And educate he did – with a life that has led him to being an amazing author and leadership veteran. Dr Munroe's success can be attributed to his Faith in his potential – he found out who he was, and he had Faith he could change his destiny based on his belief in his potential. The interesting part of his story was that the same teacher showed up at one of his leadership conferences, remarking how captivating and impactful one of his books was and sharing his regrets on the limiting words he had spoken into Dr Munroe's life.

His physical life is no more but his journey and legacy live on and his work is inspiring. Find his books and other inspiring work at https://www.munroeglobal.com.

> *Faith without work is dead, and so we need to demonstrate our belief in our potential by taking action towards it.*

Chapter Reflection

1. Identify a goal you have and lead yourself in the process of visualizing what you want to achieve from that goal. Let your imagination be as limitless as possible.
   List these thoughts.

2. Develop or find a FAITH mantra to be used in times of FEAR.
   For example, Faith it till you make it.

Chapter Nuggets

- With FAITH, all things are possible.
- Set up yourself to receive your success.
- Write your vision down and link faith to what you visualize.
- Realize the outcome is yours – OWN it.

CHAPTER 5

Don't Dim Your Light

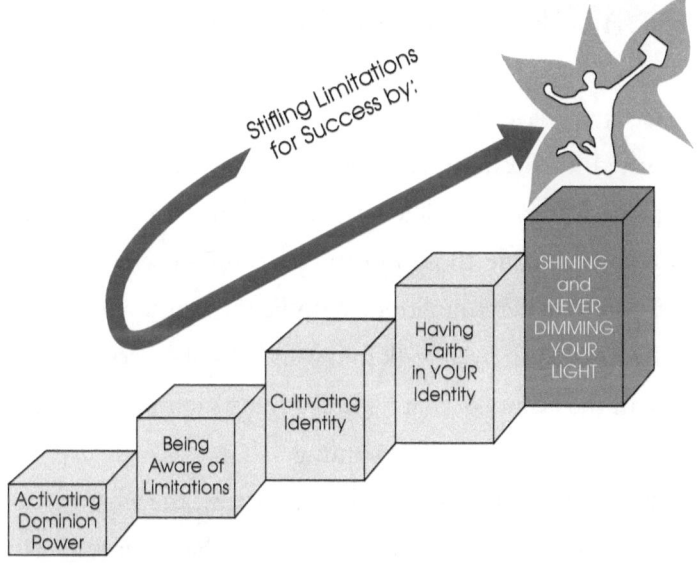

Keep Shining

The great Rudyard Kipling wrote:

> I keep six honest serving men
> (They taught me all I knew);
> Their names are What and Why and When
> And How and Where and Who.

Once you have recognized your Dominion Power and activated it, you have developed the elements necessary for awareness of your possible limitations. This awareness leads to a path to stifle those limitations through self-definition and potential determination. With Faith, your potential will be harnessed, and you walk into your light of success. As you bask in the beauty of that light, Rudyard Kipling's words are critical for you to continue shining.

It is a great strategy to outline your why, the what that is needed to accomplish that why, or the what your why will produce. Your when and how give you direction and the where and who help with expansion.

A lot of people reap the harvest but then feel intimidated to enjoy its fruit. They feel intimidated to display the fruits due to fear of judgment by others and the fear of comments by others. After you have completed the cycle of finding your light – do not dim your light for anyone or any circumstance. Let your light shine within this world of darkness.

Light speaks to:

- power
- illumination
- vision
- igniting.

Myles Munroe said, 'We cannot become what we are born to be by remaining what we are'.[1] As a result – we need to let our light shine. This light will only shine when we rebuke the darkness.

To rebuke is to express sharp disapproval against something. When you rebuke the darkness, you are sternly proclaiming that you DISAPPROVE of its presence in your life. Any odds against your light shining should be identified and dismantled. Be in the business of rebuking the darkness – darkness such as toxic people who believe you cannot live and enjoy the fruits of your potential. Darkness is like your inner critic that says you will lose friends because you are becoming too successful.

Challenge those odds and redesign your perspective. Select a diet that matches your intentions, surround yourself with the right people, and create your own connections. Do not allow people to prevent you from letting your light shine because they feel intimidated by it.

Your Keep Shining Platform

One of the ways you can keep shining is to develop a shining platform that forms the foundation of what you do and why you do it. This will be your motivation to keep shining.

Below I'll explain to you what a Keep Shining Platform is, then I'll demonstrate my Keep Shining Platform, and in the chapter reflection, I've provided space for you to create your own Keep Shining Platform.

How to Develop Your Keep Shining Platform
What do I want my potential to produce?
As you identify who you are and what you possess, you can determine what you want the impact of your defined identity to be on society. This will allow you to understand why you are passionate about the cause or service you provide. During your questioning and doubting phase in the shining period, this impact statement gives you the fire to continue since you will realize that it is not about you but the

impact your identity delivers. This helps to give you justification and a plan to arrive at that place.

Why do I want my potential to produce this?

This aspect focuses more on the emotional parameter of your identity. It allows you to attach your personal experiences – stories of others you know – to the impact you want to have. It is where you feel the cause or service over yourself. It allows you to remember that time you were abused or cheated on or conquered. That feeling pushes you to have reasoning behind the cause or service.

When do I want my ideas to be a reality?

As you project a timeline, you give yourself accountability. When you achieve the desired outcome and you reflect on the doubtful moments, it serves as a reflective evaluation of the goal attained. The journey to that goal will also help to motivate you further in the spark to continue the shine.

How do I want it to be accomplished?

Your HOW gives you the steps needed and will also be used in the reflective phase to demonstrate how the actual strategies were deviated from or accomplished, again serving as a motivational tool to continue shining.

Where will my potential be realized?
Your WHERE is your community – because of the community you serve and the needs of that community, you need to continue shining. Your community depends on you. When you know and understand who they are, you are strengthened by their need to continue your mission.

Who will my potential impact?
Your WHO is the specific people from your community – because of these people in your community that are served by you, you need to continue shining.

These questions when answered allow you to be reminded of your initial purpose to be all you wanted to be and give you reason to keep shining despite the distractions. Your Keep Shining Platform creates the basis to project your life to attain the dreams you have set. Later it acts as the reservoir that will feed your soul with continuous drive and motivation to continue being the best version of yourself and serve the world with the light you provide.

As I write this book – I am working on my own Keep Shining Framework for an initiative with young women, and I answered the questions. Use this as a guide.

What do I want my potential to produce?
Books and speaking engagements that will serve young women remarkably, to provide them with guidance:

- for creating a belief system in their potential
- to a path of self-love
- in harmonizing their lives through body, mind, heart and spirit
- to build relationships.

Why do I want my potential to produce this?
It is my belief that we all should feel we:

- are worthwhile and made for a life of abundance
- can be an exception to the rule
- can thrive and not just survive
- can live by the principle of self-definition.

This is based on my personal journey of limited self-love and the release to finding that love, and the need to encourage young women to also find that love because when you are in love with yourself, your path to living an authentic life is shorter.

When do I want my idea to be reality?
My idea will be a continuous journey annually as I create and produce resources needed to meet the goals outlined.

How do I want it to be accomplished?
Through writing, speaking and workshops that will create:

- wholeness through participation in content-rich sessions that focus on body, mind, spirit, and soul
- a sense of possibility through stifling any barriers that suppress their desire to maximize their potential
- a nutritive and transformational environment for sharing bonds as sisters.

Where will my potential be realized?
In communities, churches, Toastmasters and universities.

Who will my potential impact?
I will impact young women.

Your Keep Shining Framework forms the guide for the continuity of success in your dreams and it gives you an anchor. Do know that the platform can be developed for every idea you wish to execute so you are goal-specific in your SHINE.

We need to become someone we have not yet seen by believing in our possibilities. Step into your purpose by using your story as your fuel and not your fortification. Some of us want to operate cautiously regarding our successes, which is fine but do not be so cautious that your light eventually starts to dim. Use your journeys as strength to survive boldly – shine knowing that you will add value and be a candle to add light throughout the world. Our capacity is limitless, and we should endeavour to see how far we can grow and go.

Rise above your storms as you let your seed break forth through the comfortable soil.

Remember that you were made for so much more than an ordinary life and you can STIFLE any LIMITATION that seeks to keep you grounded in mediocrity and a purposeless life.

You are worth so much more than you give yourself credit for.

Shining can be its own form of limitation and therefore you need to be careful when you arrive at this place. Dimming your light to make others feel secure can be seen as the most convenient option, but it is the most detrimental. The world needs your gifts, talents, ideas, passion, and purpose. Your success really is not for you but for society, so you rob the world when you do not give us all you've got.

The key is to always remember that you are not to operate with pride during your shine but to use your shine to help others to find their light so they can also shine.

> *Believe this and launch out into being the best version of YOU.*

Chapter Reflection

Document your Keep Shining Framework below.

What do I want my potential to produce?

_____

_____

_____

Why do I want my potential to produce this?

_____

_____

_____

When do I want my ideas to be a reality?

_____

_____

_____

How do I want it to be accomplished?

Where will my potential be realized?

Who will my potential impact?

What do I want my potential to produce?

Chapter Nuggets

- Know your why and never forget it.
- Understand what you need to do to keep your outcome relevant, and understand the *what* your *why* will produce.
- Your *when* and *how* give you direction.
- The *where* and *who* help with expansion.
- The world needs your gifts, talents, ideas, passion and purpose, so keep on giving them.

Shine and Continue to Shine

The path to stifling limitations cannot be done alone. It is important to find examples of people who have passed through the process to motivate you that it is possible. Be aware of those who may not have succeeded and examine what their weaknesses were. This is in no way an indication of your possibility for success, so be careful not to guide your success based on their merits.

You now have the five simple steps to allow you to stifle limitations and boldly walk into your truth. Remember to always remain humble as you transition your life from stagnant to flowing.

RISE and activate your power to dominate;
    Be truthful about what your limits are;
        Find yourself through your potential and ultimately
            believe in your found truth by having;
                Faith in the revealed self then;
                    Shine and continue to shine.

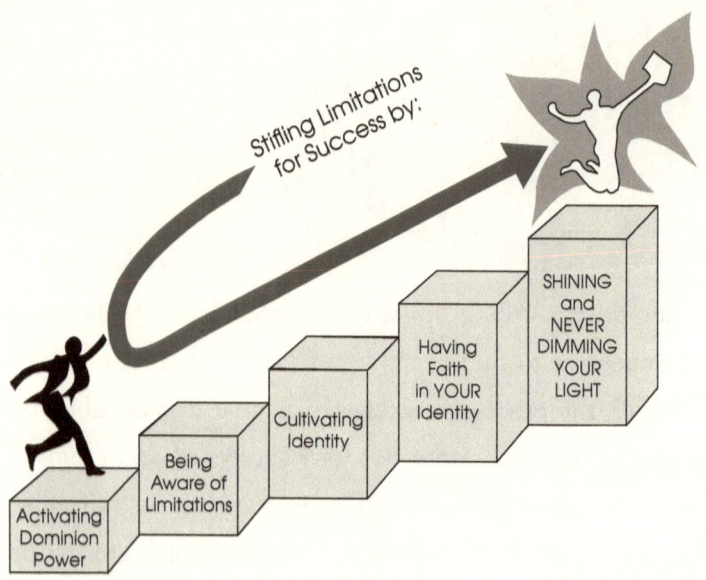

References

Chapter 1
1. *King James Version* (n.d.), Gem Publishing.
2. www.ellawheelerwilcox.org/poems/pachieve.htm.
3. *Lisa Nichols on the Steve Harvey Show* (2014), Retrieved from www.youtube.com/user/motivatingthemasses.

Chapter 2
1. Dr Myles Munroe (2003), *Maximizing Your Potential: The keys to dying empty*, Destiny Image® Publishers, Inc.

Chapter 3
1. *Thrive* (n.d.). Beach Street and Reunion Records, Retrieved from www.youtube.com/user/CastingCrowns.
2. *King James Version* (n.d.), Gem Publishing.

Chapter 4
1. *King James Version* (n.d.), Gem Publishing.
2. Dr Myles Munroe, 'My Life Story' from JKL Show (2018), Retrieved from www.youtube.com/watch?v=EjVqmpGmbuw

Chapter 5
1. Dr Myles Munroe (2003), *Maximizing Your Potential: The keys to dying empty*, Destiny Image® Publishers, Inc.

Notes

Notes

Notes

Notes

Notes